WHERE THE F*CK ARE MY KEYS?!

WHERE THE F*CK ARE MY KEYS?!

HUGH JASSBURN

Find them—

WE'VE ALL BEEN THERE: BUSY DAY AHEAD, RUNNING LATE, BUT NO SIGN OF YOUR MISSING KEYS! JUST WHERE THE F*CK HAVE THEY GONE? WHAT WOULD NORMALLY INDUCE ALL KINDS OF RAGE IN REAL LIFE CAN NOW BE A SOURCE OF MENTAL STIMULATION AND AMUSEMENT WITH THE HELP OF THIS COMICAL COLLECTION OF VISUAL PUZZLES. FIND YOUR KEYS IN A RANGE OF EVERYDAY AND NOT-SO-EVERYDAY ENVIRONMENTS —AND TRY NOT TO SWEAR.

FIND THEM IN THE CUTLERY DRAWER

DID YOU DROP THEM IN THE SOCK PILE?

ARE THEY IN YOUR TOOL BOX?

GET IN WITH THE CREEPY-CRAWLIES

YOU DROPPED THEM IN THE TRASH CAN!

FIND THEM IN THE BATTERIES BOX

SEARCH AMONG THE BULBS

DID YOU DROP THEM IN THE GARBAGE?

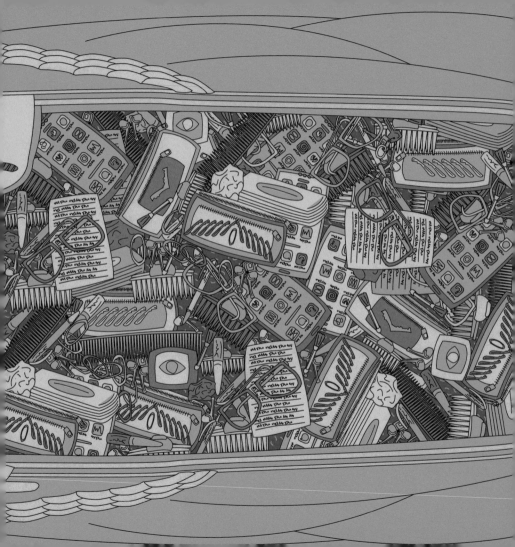

SEARCH YOUR BATHROOM CABINET

FIND THEM IN THE FLOWER BED

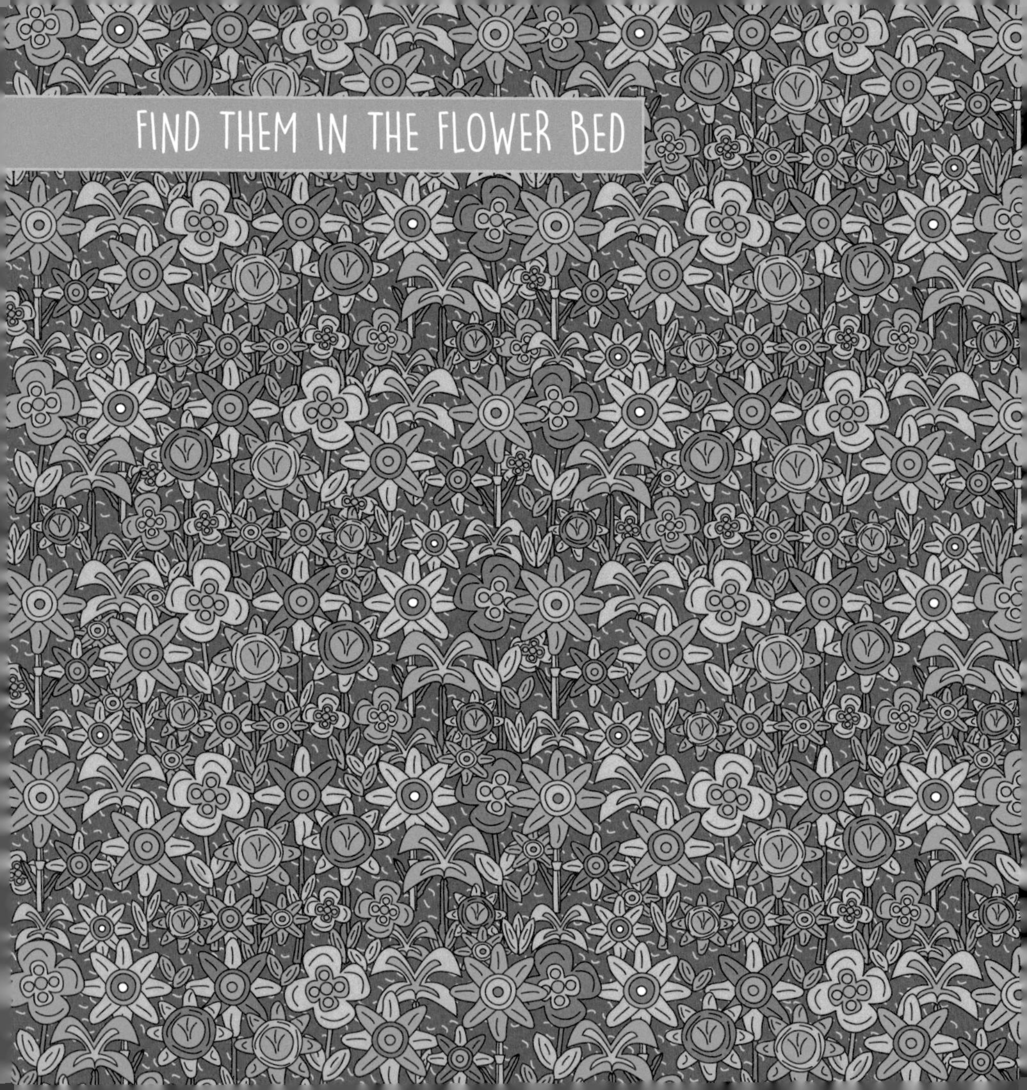

ARE THEY IN THE CLEANING CUPBOARD?

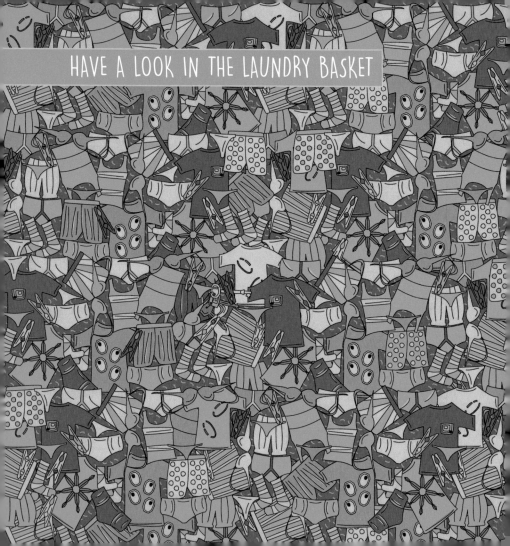

HAVE A LOOK IN THE LAUNDRY BASKET

FIND THEM IN THE FRUIT BOWL

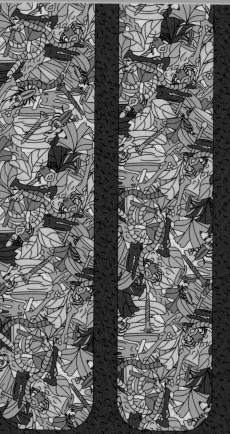

YOU DROPPED THEM DOWN A DRAIN!

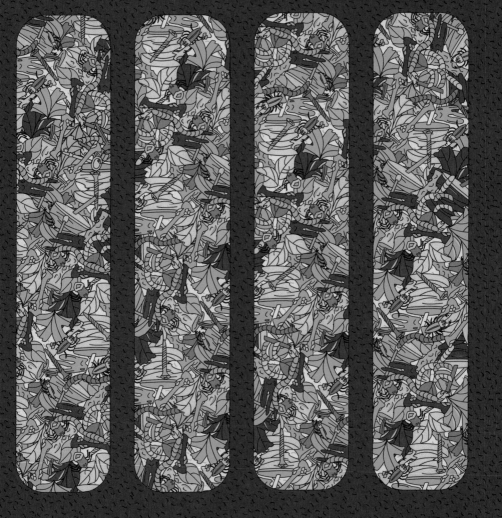

DID YOU LEAVE THEM IN THE GARDEN SHED?

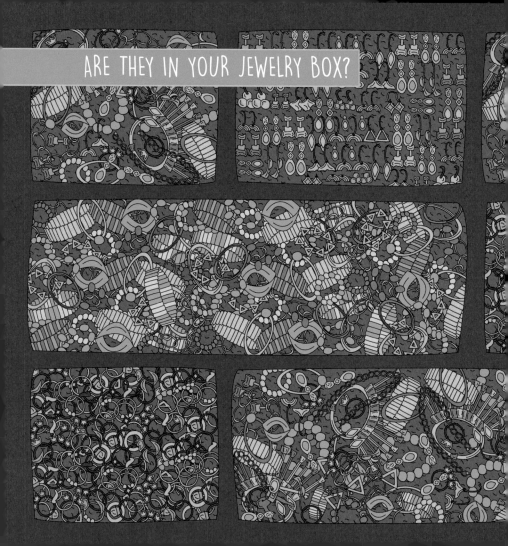

ARE THEY IN YOUR JEWELRY BOX?

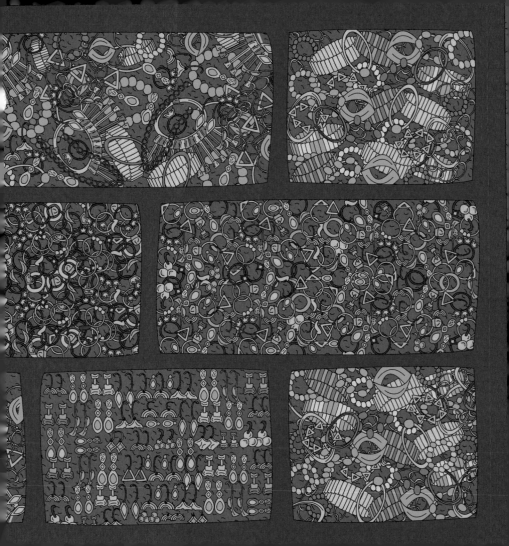

DID YOU DROP THEM ON THE BEACH?

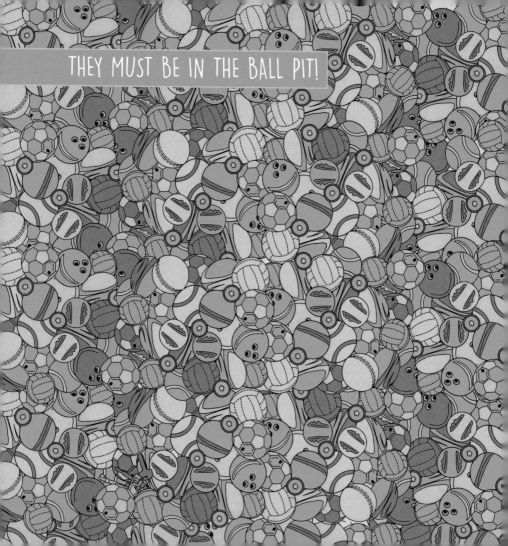

THEY MUST BE IN THE BALL PIT!

GET YOUR HANDS WET!

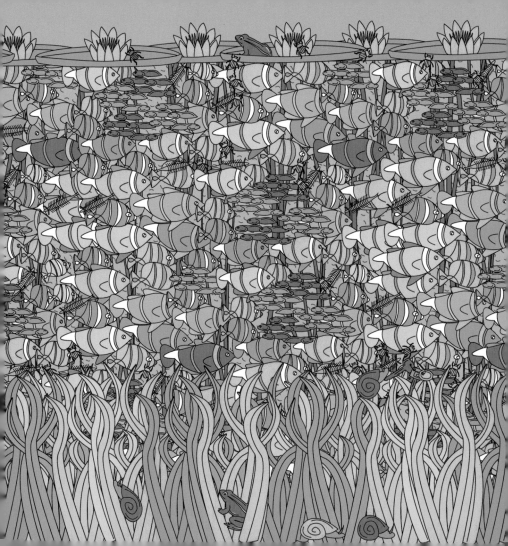

DOWN THE BACK OF THE COUCH?

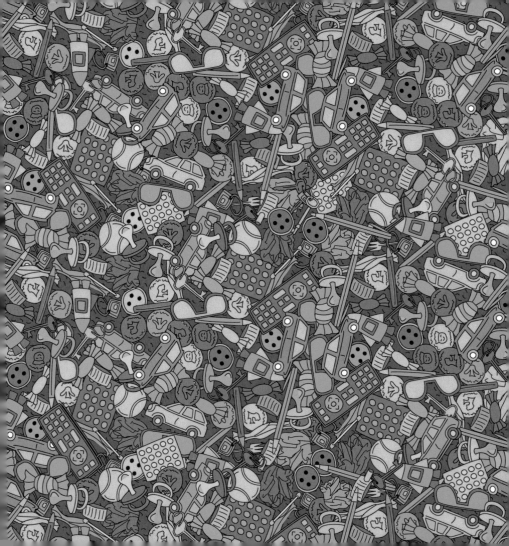

HOW ABOUT THE TOY CUPBOARD?

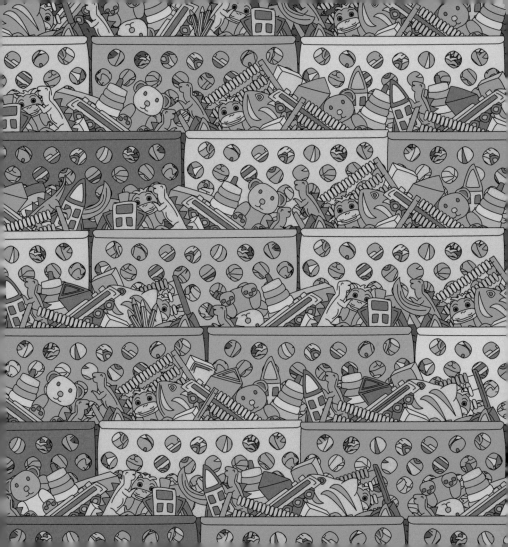

YOU DROPPED THEM IN A SNAKE PIT!

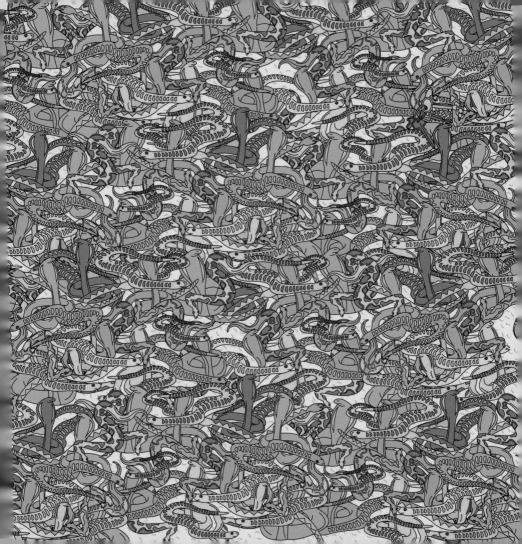

ARE THEY AT THE GOLF CLUB?

OR AT THE BOOKSTORE?

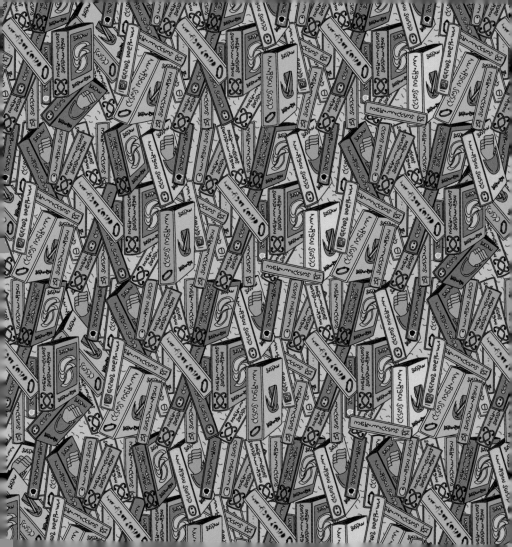

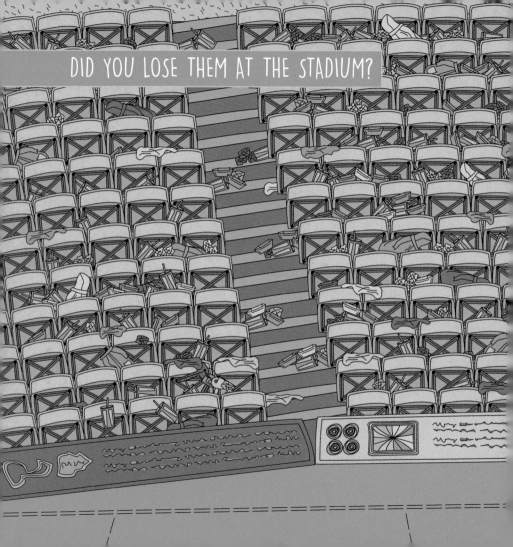

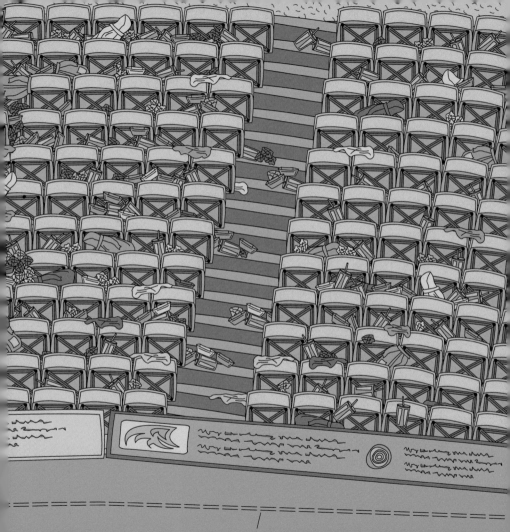

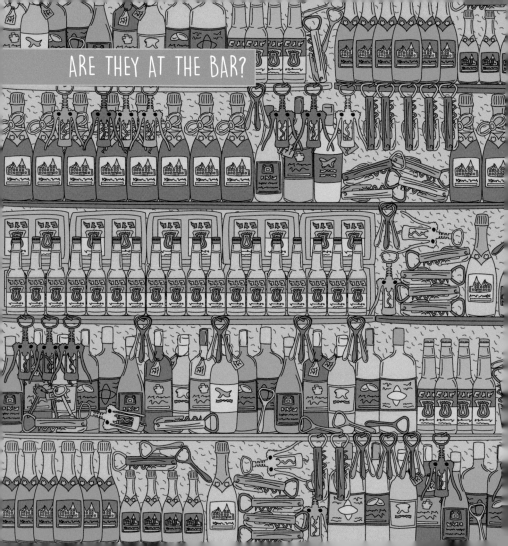

ARE THEY AT THE BAR?

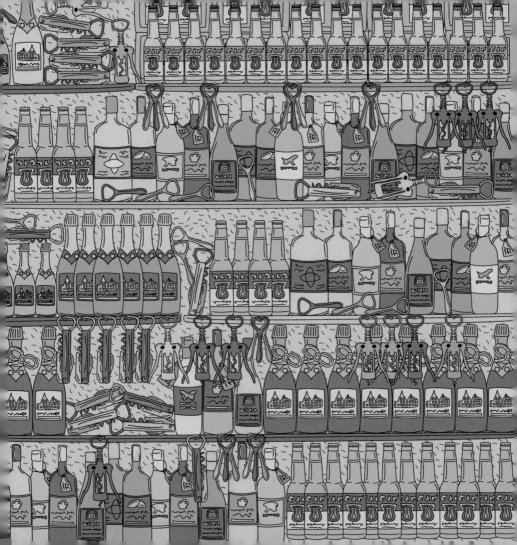

THEY MUST BE IN OUTER SPACE!

YOU DROPPED THEM ON THE SKI TRAIL!

THE MAGPIE MUST HAVE TAKEN THEM!

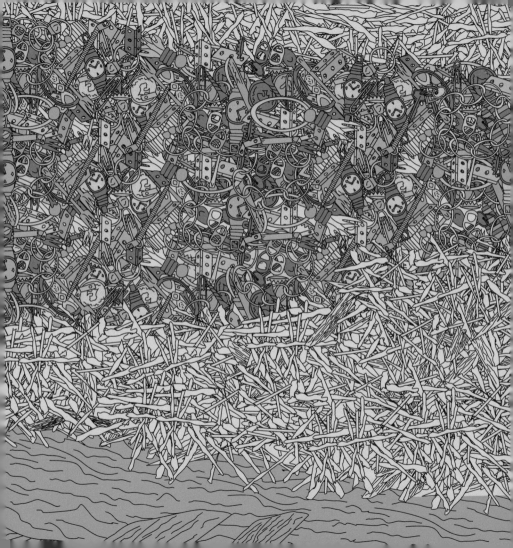

TRY SOME MEDITATION...

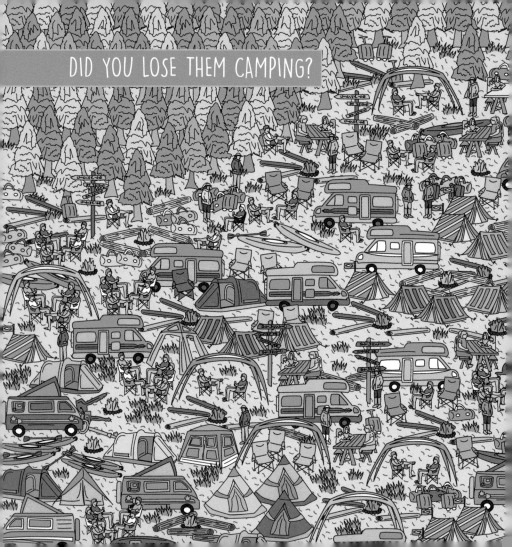

DID YOU LOSE THEM CAMPING?

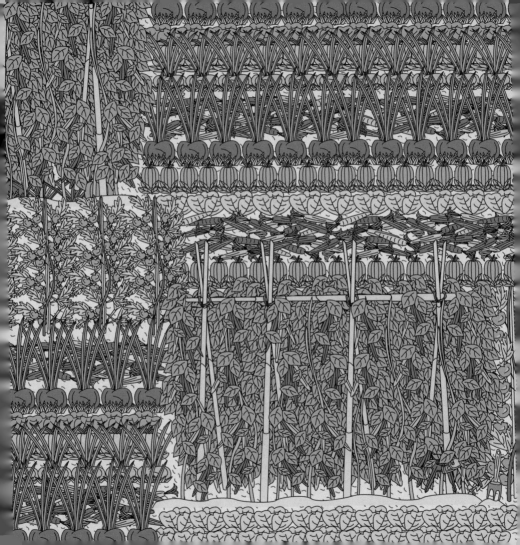

TRY THE SHOE STORE

RUMMAGE AMONG THE WATCHES

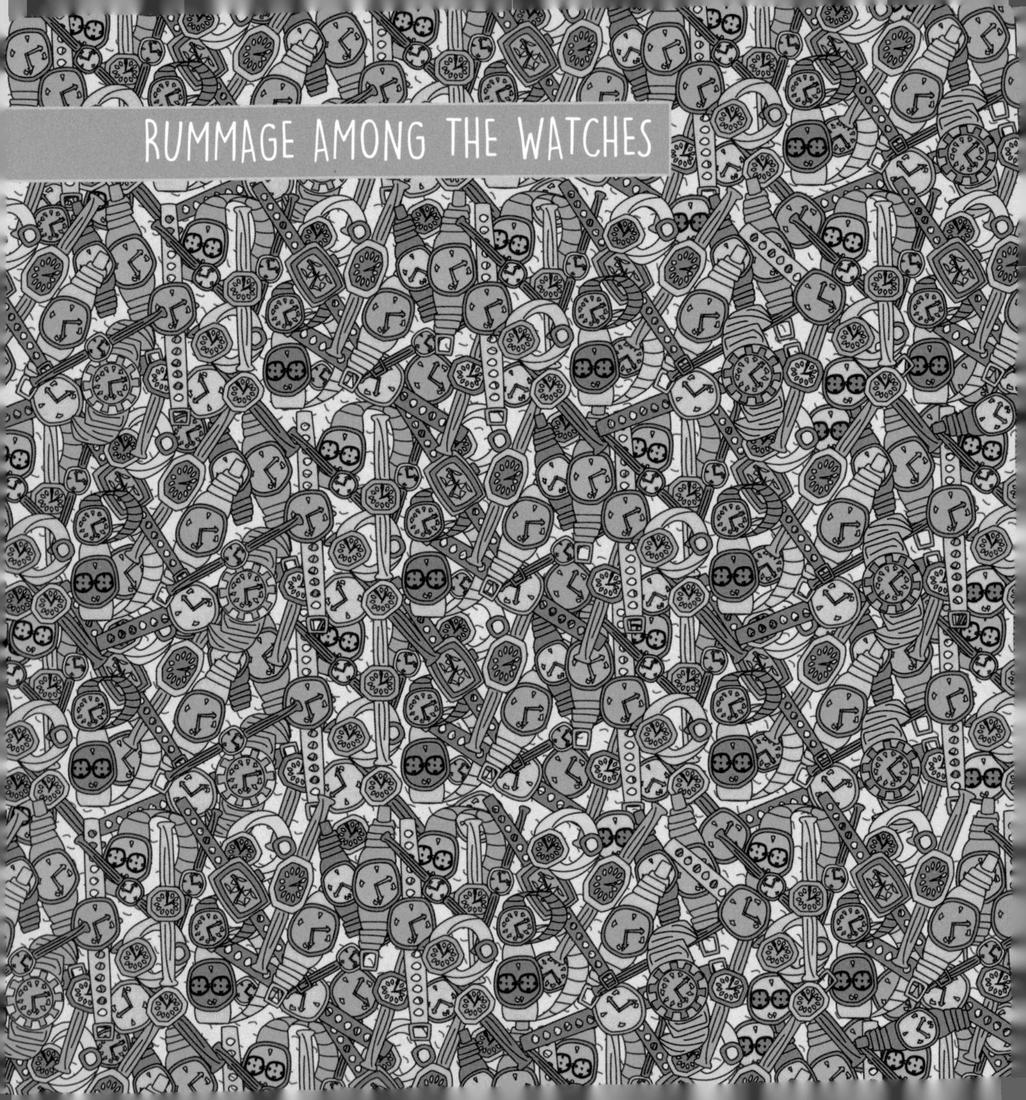

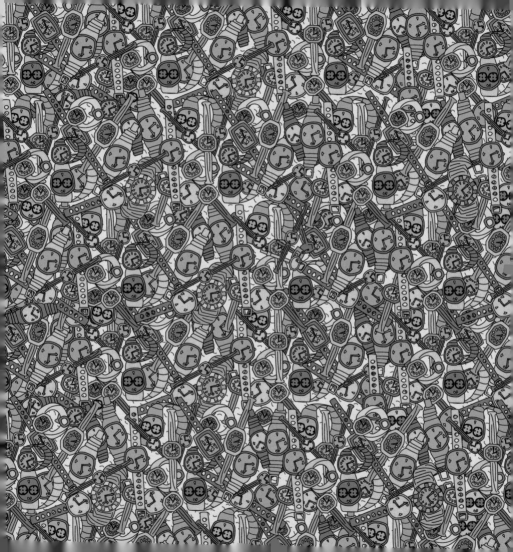

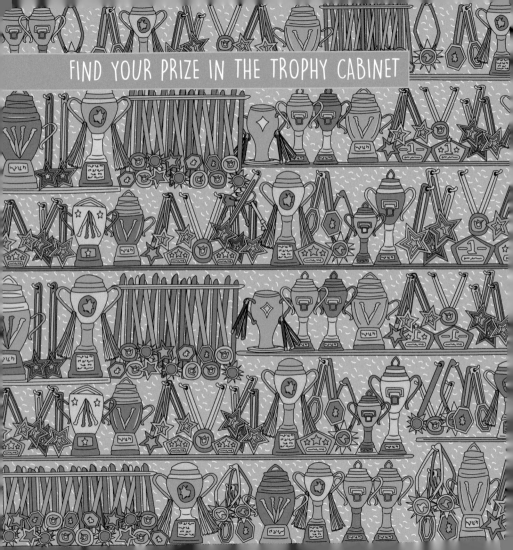

FIND YOUR PRIZE IN THE TROPHY CABINET

ARE THEY HAUNTING THE HALLOWEEN PARTY?

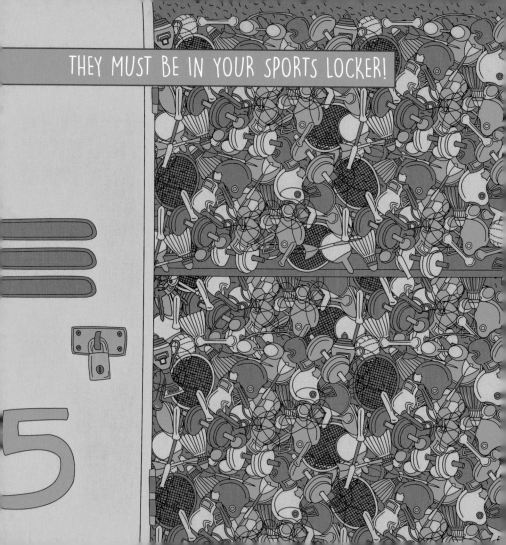

THEY MUST BE IN YOUR SPORTS LOCKER!

5

FIND THEM IN THE CUTLERY DRAWER

DID YOU DROP THEM IN THE SOCK PILE?

RUMMAGE AMONG THE POTTED PLANTS

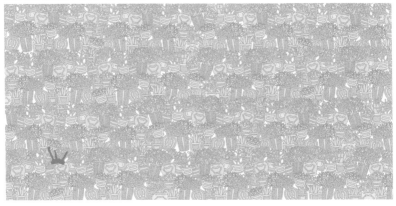

ARE THEY IN YOUR TOOL BOX?

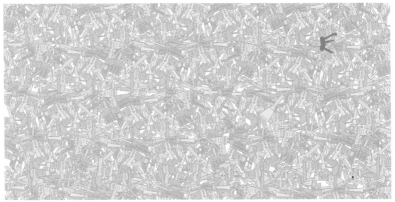

GET IN WITH THE CREEPY-CRAWLIES

YOU DROPPED THEM IN THE TRASH CAN!

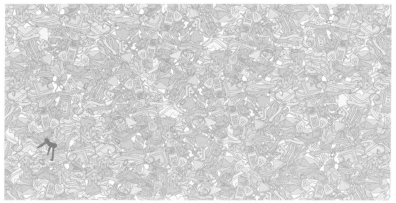

FIND THEM IN THE BATTERIES BOX

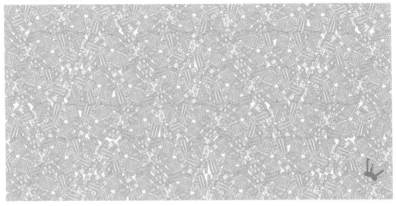

SEARCH AMONG THE BULBS

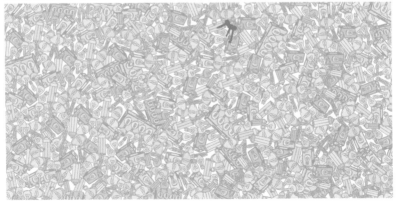

DID YOU DROP THEM IN THE GARBAGE?

ARE THEY IN YOUR HANDBAG?

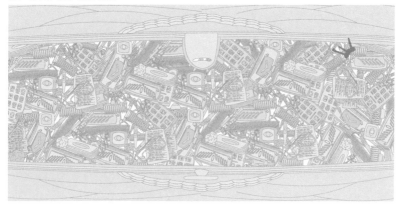

SEARCH YOUR BATHROOM CABINET

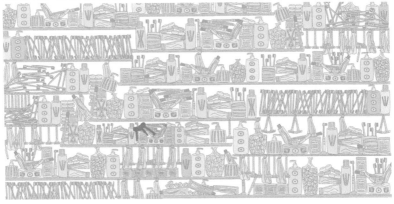

FIND THEM IN THE FLOWER BED

ARE THEY IN THE CLEANING CUPBOARD?

HAVE A LOOK IN THE LAUNDRY BASKET

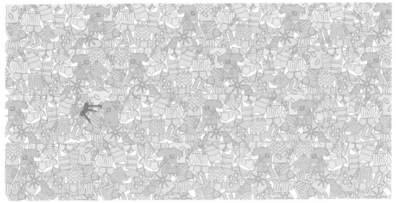

FIND THEM IN THE FRUIT BOWL

YOU DROPPED THEM DOWN A DRAIN!

DID YOU LEAVE THEM IN THE GARDEN SHED?

HOW ABOUT THE COFFEE SHOP?

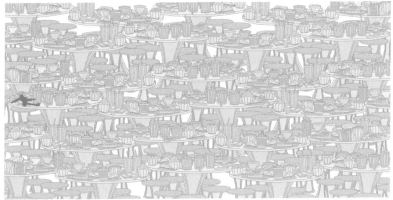

ARE THEY IN YOUR JEWELRY BOX?

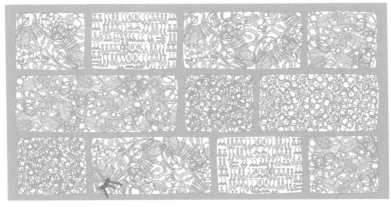

DID YOU DROP THEM ON THE BEACH?

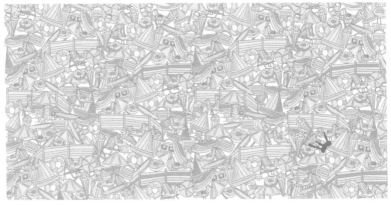

THEY MUST BE IN THE BALL PIT!

GET YOUR HANDS WET!

DID YOU LEAVE THEM AT THE OFFICE?

DOWN THE BACK OF THE COUCH?

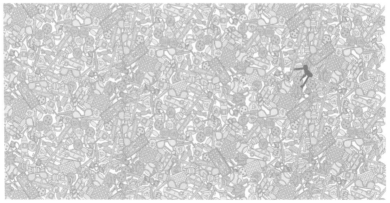

HOW ABOUT THE TOY CUPBOARD?

YOU DROPPED THEM IN A SNAKE PIT!

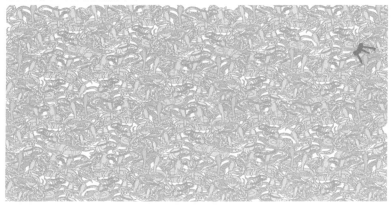

ARE THEY AT THE GOLF CLUB?

OR AT THE BOOKSTORE?

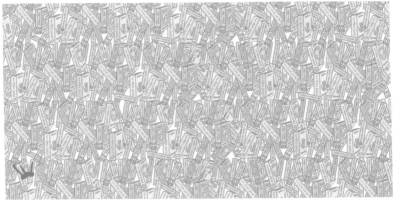

DID YOU LOSE THEM AT THE STADIUM?

ARE THEY AT THE BAR?

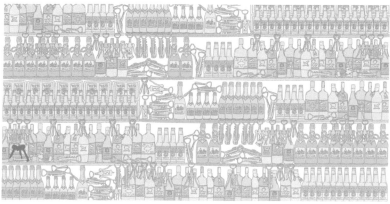

THEY MUST BE IN OUTER SPACE!

YOU DROPPED THEM ON THE SKI TRAIL!

THE MAGPIE MUST HAVE TAKEN THEM!

TRY SOME MEDITATION. . .

DID YOU LOSE THEM CAMPING?

FIND THEM IN THE VEG PATCH

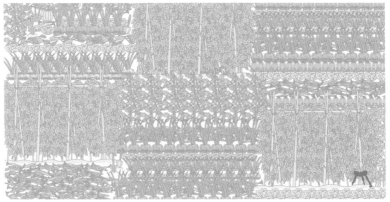

TRY THE SHOE STORE

RUMMAGE AMONG THE WATCHES

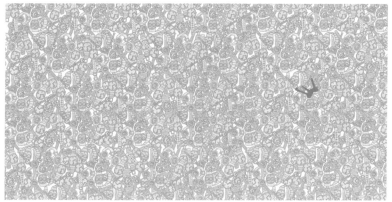

FIND YOUR PRIZE IN THE TROPHY CABINET

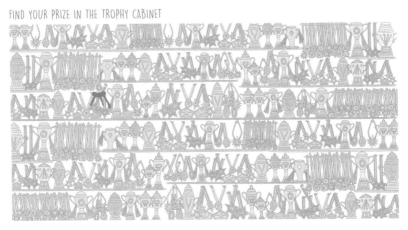

YOU DROPPED THEM IN THE PARKING LOT!

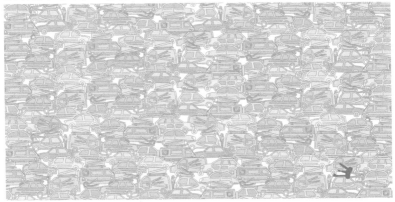

ARE THEY HAUNTING THE HALLOWEEN PARTY?

THEY MUST BE IN YOUR SPORTS LOCKER!